New Life in Christ

A Manual for Membership Classes
in Mennonite Brethren Churches

by Herb Kopp

KINDRED
PRODUCTIONS

New Life in Christ

Second printing of 2011 revision: June 2017

Published by Kindred Productions, Winnipeg, MB R3M 3Z6.

Cover and book design by Audrey Plew

Leader's Guide by Michael Dick, Abbotsford, BC

Printed in Canada by Friesens, Altona, MB
International Standard Book Number: 978-0-921788-24-9

Table of Contents

A Life of Service
Spiritual gifts
Finding and developing your gift/s

A Life of Witness
Overcoming fear
The gospel: In word and deed

Describing the community of faith
The purpose of the church
Why be part of a local church?
Discipline in the church
Giving and receiving in the church

Expressing the Covenant Community: Baptism
The meaning of the word "baptize".
A sign of incorporation into the church
Issues facing persons considering baptism

Expressing the Covenant Community: The Lord's Supper
The historical setting of the Lord's Supper
Jesus, the disciples and the Passover meal
The meaning of Jesus' communion words
What does this mean for us?
Who is invited to the Lord's Table?

The Anabaptist movement
Mennonite Brethren origins
The Mennonite Brethren Church today
Doing together what we can't do alone

Preface

The commitment Jesus made to his disciples was that he would build his church. The commission he gave the church was to make disciples.

Growing up towards Christ-likeness is possible only after becoming a spiritually new person. That new birth is the result of believing in and receiving Jesus Christ as Saviour and Lord in our lives. God performs the miracle of spiritual new birth, and then we are invited to cooperate with him as the live-in Holy Spirit leads and empowers us to grow from infancy to maturity in our New Life in Christ.

Historically, Mennonite Brethren have been committed to discipleship training and baptismal preparation. "Becoming Disciples" was first published in 1968. A subsequent revision arrived in 1973. The copy in your hands was first released in 1995 and updated in 2011 with scripture references from TNIV and new information about the Mennonite Brethren family.

Many thanks to author Herb Kopp for his excellent work, and Michael Dick for the Leader's Guide.

New Life in Christ is intended to help Mennonite Brethren churches make basic discipleship classes positive and meaningful experiences. The content is not exhaustive, but we commend it to the church as a helpful guide for leader and learner in classes preparing believers for baptism and church membership, and also in other appropriate discipleship studies. As disciples are made, Jesus will indeed be building his church. It's our enthusiastic prayer that God will be honoured as this resource and your conversation enhances your life in Christ.

The Board of Faith and Life

chapter one
Beginning the new life

The Bible is very clear about the need for all persons to become Christians. To become a Christian means that we have received new life in Christ. There are many ways of speaking about this new life, but they all describe the same event. The language we use to describe this event is less important than the fact that it has occurred. What is most important is that we have entered into an authentic relationship with God through Christ.

The words we use to describe salvation

The church has spoken about a relationship with God for many centuries, so many of the words used to describe this relationship are very old, yet they remain rich in meaning. We speak about "being a Christian", having "received Christ as Saviour", having been "saved" or "converted", having "repented of sins", having "believed in Jesus", having been "regenerated" and having become "a follower of Jesus Christ".

Similarly, the Gospel of John uses several metaphors to describe salvation, each addressing a particular need in life. Salvation is spoken of as being "born again" (John 3); as having received "the water of life" (John 4); as having eaten "the bread of life" (John 6); as having "followed the light" (John 8); as having entered "the sheep fold" (John 10); and as having been grafted into "the vine" (John 15).

There are many other words and metaphors which describe what it means to have become a Christian. What is common is that all of these things signify a gift from God to us.

Everyone needs salvation

The Bible teaches that without an authentic relationship with God through Christ, it is not possible to enter the Kingdom of God. The problem is our alienation from God through sin. When God created the first people, Adam and Eve, he created them perfect and without sin (Genesis 1:26-27), but it didn't take long before both Adam and Eve had succumbed to the temptation of Satan and disobeyed God (Genesis 2:16-17; 3:1ff).

In this act of disobedience a vast gulf between God and humanity came into being. The excuses Adam and Eve made to cover up their disobedience were unacceptable (Genesis 3:12-13). Therefore, God banished them to a life characterized by hard work, pain and alienation from himself, followed by the ultimate penalty, death (Genesis 3:16-19; Romans 6:23; John 3:18, 36). All human beings, because of Adam and Eve's disobedience, are now contaminated by sin (Romans 5:12). Not only are all persons born with a tendency toward sin (Psalm 51:5), but they also practice sin every day (Romans 3:23; I John 1:8).

Some people think that they can change themselves and become good enough to meet God's requirements for salvation. It is true that we can live relatively good lives, but this does not answer the problem of our sinfulness.

We need to know two important things about sin. First, the primary problem isn't so much with the sin-things we do; rather, the problem is that we are, by nature, sinful. Sin has enslaved us; it has contaminated us at the core of our being. Therefore, sin has power over us, and we are helpless in this condition. We sin, not necessarily because we want to sin, but rather because we are controlled by a sinful nature (Romans 7:5). If we are to receive salvation, this deeply rooted problem of sin must be addressed. Without a fundamental change in our nature, we cannot be "saved".

Second is the matter of the sin-things we do. The sins we commit (actions, words, thoughts) are a symptom of our alienation from God. The root cause of sinning is our sinful nature; the symptoms of our alienation from God are the sins which we commit.

Salvation is the answer to our sinfulness

The answer to this terrible problem of being controlled by our sinful nature is salvation. Salvation has two important parts to it.

First, the problem of our sinful nature is answered by our receiving salvation from God as a gift (Ephesians 2:8 - 9). This is the only remedy for our sinful nature (Romans 8:1 - 4). There is no way to break the stranglehold sin has on us, except through the gift of salvation which comes through Christ. This is what the Bible means when it says: "Believe in the Lord Jesus and you will be saved" (Acts 16:31); and "Salvation is found in no one else, for there is no other name givenunder heaven by which we must be saved" (Acts 4:12).

Second, when the power of sin has been broken through the gift of salvation, we are able to deal with the sins we commit day by day.

Although these two parts of salvation appear to drive a wedge between "salvation as a gift" and "salvation as a changed life", they are, in fact, very closely related. In Jesus Christ the stranglehold of sin is broken, and therefore we are able to live changed lives. In Christ, salvation and ethics (that is, how we live) come together (Galatians 5:16-26).

What happens when we receive the gift of salvation?

Though salvation is a cooperative affair between human beings and God, it always begins with God. He awakens in us the desire to have a relationship with him — a relationship which bridges the gulf that our sinfulness has created.

It is important to note that though our sinfulness has caused a serious breach in relationship with God, the situation is not hopeless. We are not hopelessly lost; we are simply helplessly lost. God's love comes to us while we are still in our helpless state (John 3:16; Romans 5:8); he bridges the gulf between us.

Therefore, salvation is God reaching toward us with his love. We, in turn, respond to this love by accepting his gift of salvation.

When we accept the gift of salvation, at least five things happen to us.

We are reconciled to God. This reconciliation can happen because God has taken the initiative by sending his Son, Jesus Christ, to be born a human being (John 3:16; Hebrews 1:2-3; 2 Corinthians 5:18-20). Jesus Christ, being God himself, became a human so that he might, by his life, death and resurrection, redeem humanity. He, unlike us, was born without sin and lived a life without sin (2 Corinthians 5:21). He died so that we do not have to suffer eternally for our sinfulness. God accepted Jesus' sinless life and his death as an acceptable offering for our sinfulness (Romans 3:22-26; 1 John 2:2).

We are set free. Through Christ's death, God defeated Satan, who had gained control of all of humanity through the sin of Adam and Eve (2 Corinthians 4:4; 1 John 5:19). In Christ, God reversed the damage that Adam and Eve inflicted on humanity (Romans 5:12-19). Through the atoning sacrifice of Christ, the power of sin was broken, and we are now able to become "a new creation" in Christ Jesus (2 Corinthians 5:17).

We have received Christ's righteousness as a gift (2 Corinthians 5:21); that is, we are declared to be righteous by God himself (Romans 3:22-26). Therefore, there is now "no condemnation" to those who have been set free by Christ (Romans 8:1 - 4). Salvation is freedom — freedom from slavery to sin and freedom to serve God and our fellow human beings (Galatians 5:1,13).

We are forgiven. Not only have we been declared to be righteous, we are also forgiven the sin-things which we have done, and which we continue to do. The key lies in asking for and accepting the continuing forgiveness of God. (1 John 1:9; Matthew 6:12).

Earlier we noted that there are two significant things about sin: the sinful nature with which we all are born and, second, the sins we commit. God's salvation is the answer to both of these problems. Through reconciliation we are made new in Christ, all old things having passed away (2 Corinthians 5:17); through forgiveness God blots from our record the sins which we have committed.

We are united in Christ and incorporated into his body, the church. Through the gift of salvation the new Christian becomes "a partaker of the divine nature" (2 Peter 1:4). This cuts two ways: first, we are said to be "in Christ" (John 14:20; 15:4; 1 Corinthians 12:27; Colossians 3:1–4); and, second, God is said to be in us (1 Corinthians 3:16; 6:19; Romans 8:9). The presence of God within us is through the indwelling Holy Spirit.

We receive the gift of the Holy Spirit. At Pentecost (Acts 2:1ff) the Holy Spirit, as promised by Jesus himself (John 16:5-16) and as prophesied by John the Baptist (Luke 3:15-18), came to live in the infant church. The Holy Spirit is given to each person as that person becomes a believer and is united to Christ (Romans 8:9b-10). The Holy Spirit is the seal of God's approval on us (Ephesians 1:13-14.)

Accepting the gift of salvation

A gift, by definition, is something that comes to us through the generosity of the giver. We cannot demand it; nor can we work for it. All we can do is either accept or refuse it. Our part in salvation is accepting the gift.

Acceptance as receiving Christ. The gift of salvation bridges the gulf which exists between God and sinful humanity, and, in accepting salvation, we acknowledge our need to be reconciled to God. We accept this gift by faith, and the gift is Christ himself. We receive Christ (John 1:12), and, in receiving Christ, we receive salvation (Ephesians 2:8-9).

Acceptance as an indication of repentance. To repent means to have great sorrow over our sinfulness and to have the willingness to forsake it. To "repent" literally means to "turn around" -- that is, to turn from our sinful life and to turn to Christ as our Saviour. It describes a willingness to leave our old life behind and to begin a new life with Christ. Again and again Jesus and his disciples called for repentance (Mark 1:15; Acts 2:38; Luke 18:9-14; 19:1-10).

Acceptance as confession of Christ. The person who has received this gift of salvation is now a part of God's family, the church. This calls for a public confession of this new relationship.

Both Jesus (Matthew 10:32-33) and Paul (Romans 10:9-10) called for a bold witness to the new life in Christ.

How do we know we have received the gift of salvation?

Some persons, when they receive the gift of salvation, have a strong emotional sense that new life has begun within them. For others, this feeling is less pronounced. For still others, it never comes. Salvation is never a matter of "feeling", though feeling isn't unusual; salvation must be based on the solid foundation of "knowing" for certain that it has happened. Frequently, new Christians, and even some more mature Christians, ask the question: "How can I know that I have received Christ when I don't feel it?" Here are three ways to know that salvation has come to you:

Assurance of salvation as trust. The Bible says that to have Christ as Saviour is to have eternal life (1 John 5:12). The only condition to "having" Christ is to have placed your trust in him and to have received him as Saviour (John 1:12). The question then becomes: "Have you received Christ, and are you trusting in him?" If the answer is yes, then you can be sure that you are saved (1 John 4:15; 5:1).

Assurance of salvation and the Holy Spirit. Accepting Christ means that the Holy Spirit has taken up residence within our inner being (1 Corinthians 6:19-20). To be made new is not a noisy, external thing which we can feel and hear; rather, it is a quiet internal revolution. This same Holy Spirit, who came to live in us when we received the gift of salvation, is God's abiding and energizing presence within us. The Holy Spirit, deeply and profoundly, assures us that we are the children of God (Romans 8:16).

Assurance of salvation and the changed life. When a person has come into the family of God through the gift of salvation, when the power of sin has been broken and sins have been forgiven, and when the Holy Spirit has taken up residence within, a changed life should become evident. In the letter he wrote to an early group of believers, John the Apostle began a whole series of sentences with the phrase: "This is how we know...." We can know that we are believers in Jesus Christ if we keep God's commands (1 John 2:3); keep his word (2:5); love the brothers and sisters of the church (3:14; 4:7,8,12,16); and do what is right (2:29; 3:9).

What John the Apostle is not saying is that in the keeping of these things we will be saved; rather, he is saying that in keeping these things we show that we have been saved. In other words, doing good deeds and living a good life will not save us; but, having been saved will lead to the living of a good life and to the doing of good deeds (Ephesians 2:8-10).

A Summary of Christian Teaching

God: Father, Son and Holy Spirit. There is one God, who is Father, Son and Holy Spirit (John 1:18; 1 John 4:12; John 4:24). Each person in the Godhead, though they are one, sometimes acts independently.

God is a Spirit, invisible to the eye (John 1:18; 1 John 4:12; John 4:24). God is everywhere, knows all things, and is all powerful (Psalm 139). God is holy (Isaiah 57:15; Psalm 99:9), loving (1 John 4:8-16), unchangeable (Malachi 3:6; James 1:17; Hebrews 13:8) and merciful (Psalm 103:8; Luke 15:11-32).

Jesus is God-become-man (John 1:1-4, 18), born of the virgin Mary (Luke 1:35), fully God and fully human. He lived a sinless life and became God's atonement for our sins (2 Corinthians 5:21). He lived, died for our sins, was raised to life and returned to his Father in heaven. (1 Timothy 3:16).

The **Holy Spirit** is the presence of Jesus (2 Corinthians 1:21-22) guaranteeing that we are Christ's possession (2 Corinthians 5:5). The Holy Spirit was given to the church at Pentecost (Acts 2) and lives in every believing person (1 Corinthians 6:19). The Holy Spirit convinces people that they are sinners (John 16:8) and is the "paraclete" -- the One who comes alongside to help us (Romans 8:14-26).

Humanity. God, who is a Spirit, created the human being male and female (Genesis 2:7, 20-25; 5:1-2). He created them sinless beings, in his own image (Genesis 5:1-2). There is more to the human person than that which is visible. The visible part is called the body; the invisible part is called the soul and/ or spirit. When a person dies, the body decays, but the spirit lives on forever. The believing person goes into the presence of God (2 Corinthians 5:8), while the ones who have not believed are punished forever (Revelation 20:12, 15; John 5:28-29).

Sin: the blight that distorts everything. Sin started with Satan (Ezekiel 28:15). The first people, Adam and Eve, sinned by giving in to the temptation that they would be like God (Genesis 3). Through that act, sin entered the human race and has contaminated every human person (Romans 5:12). Sin can be defined as coming short of God's standard of righteousness (Romans 3:23). Human beings sin, not necessarily because they want to sin, but because it is their nature (Jeremiah 17:9; Isaiah 53:6). The tendency to sin is passed from one generation to another, parent to child (Psalm 51:5). The penalty for sin is physical and spiritual death (Romans 6:23). Of the two deaths, spiritual death is much more to be feared than physical death (Matthew 10:28; Revelation 20:14).

Sometimes the Bible speaks of the depravity of humanity (Romans 3:10-18). This does not mean that every human being is necessarily very sinful. It does mean that all sinners are powerless to make themselves acceptable to God through their own efforts (Ephesians 2:1-3).

Salvation: God's wonderful work of recreation. Sin is the gaping chasm which separates God and humanity. The only way this gulf can be bridged is by accepting God's gift of grace, through faith in Jesus Christ. No amount of goodness or good deeds can bridge this vast chasm between God and humanity.

The Holy Spirit begins the process by convincing men and women of their sin. When they respond to this nudging of the Spirit and by faith accept God's provision for their sin, God gives new life to them (Acts 2:37; John 3:5-16).

God's side of salvation is called "regeneration", giving eternal life to the new believer (John 3:5). Humanity's side of salvation is called "conversion", which literally means "to turn around". Through conversion, a person turns from the old ways to a new life (1 Thessalonians 1:9). This work, deep within the heart of a person, cannot be seen (John 3:8), but the new life which issues from conversion is full of good works (Ephesians 2:10) and can be seen.

When persons come to God and receive salvation in Christ, they are declared to be righteous; they are "justified" (Romans 5:1, 18). The penalty for sin has been borne by Jesus Christ (1 Peter 2:24), and Christ's righteousness is granted to the new believing person (2 Corinthians 5:21).

The Scriptures assure us that God is able to keep safely those who come to him in faith (Romans 8:35-39; John 10:28-29) and give stern warnings about the dangers of sin in the life of the believer (Hebrews 3:12; 6:4-6).

Future events: Christ will return! The Bible teaches that Jesus may return at any moment and that this coming will be sudden and without warning (Matthew 24:36-44). When Jesus comes, those who have died as believing persons will be resurrected, and those who are alive at his coming will be transformed. Together they will be united with the Lord (1 Corinthians 15:15-57; 1 Thessalonians 4:13-18). Then there will come a great day of giving account for all of life. The unbelieving will face the consequences of their choice not to accept God's gift of grace (Revelation 20:4-6,11-15); the believing will receive their rewards for service (2 Corinthians 5:10; Romans 14:10; Matthew 25:41-46).

NOTES:

chapter two
Reading and understanding the Bible

Whenever renewal has occurred within the church, there has also been a renewed interest in reading, studying and applying the teachings of the Bible (also called "the Scriptures" and "the Word of God"). Not only is the Bible necessary for new life in Christ (1 Peter 1:23), but through it we also grow in faith and maturity (Acts 20:32).

The Bible as a book

The Bible is actually a collection of 66 different books, written by many different persons over a long period of time. While the exact date of writing of each of these books cannot be known with accuracy, they nonetheless fall into a period of approximately a thousand years.

The Bible is comprised of two major blocks called the Old Testament (39 books) and the New Testament (27 books). The Old Testament writings are the Scriptures of the Hebrew nation, written before the birth of Jesus Christ. The New Testament was written after the death, resurrection and ascension of Jesus. While primary attention in the church is focused on the New Testament, the two testaments together are the Scriptures for the church.

The Old Testament. The authors of some of the Old Testament books are known because they identify themselves at the beginning of their writings; others are unknown. Some books, such as the Proverbs (see 1:1; 30:1; 31:1) and the Psalms, have different authors.

The Old Testament is written largely in the Hebrew language, with some sections written in Aramaic. The New Testament is written in Greek. The English Bibles which we read today are all translations of the Hebrew/Aramaic and Greek originals.

The Hebrews divided their Scriptures into three main categories. There was the Torah, which means "the Law". This section is comprised of the first five books of the Old Testament, commonly called the Pentateuch. The names of these five books (Genesis, Exodus, Leviticus, Numbers and Deuteronomy) were derived from the first words of each of these writings.

The second division of the Old Testament was called Nebhi'im, which means "the Prophets". The "former prophets" are Joshua, Judges, Samuel and the Kings, while the "latter prophets" are Isaiah, Jeremiah, Ezekiel and the Twelve (that is, the twelve Minor Prophets, the last 12 Old Testament books in our Bibles).

The third major division, called Kethubhim, which means "the Writings", included all the rest of the Old Testament.

The Old Testament is not in chronological order; that is, the books are not in the same order as the events they describe occurred in history.

The New Testament. All of the New Testament writings were completed by approximately the end of the first century A.D., and, with the exception of the Epistle to the Hebrews, the authors of all of the New Testament writings are known.

There are three major divisions in the New Testament. The first division includes the four Gospels, which describe the life and teachings of Jesus. The authors were very diverse: a disciple (John), a tax collector (Matthew), a Gentile doctor (Luke) and a missionary drop-out (John Mark). The Book of Acts is the second volume written by Luke (See Luke 1:1-4 and Acts 1:1-2).

The second group are the Letters, written by Paul, Peter, John, James and Jude. These letters gave guidance to the fledgling churches which were encountering difficulty. Though these letters have theological teaching within them, they have been described as "theology on the fly"; they are really pastoral, missionary letters. Only Romans and Hebrews reflect deliberate theological thought.

The third group is called Apocalyptic literature. Though there is only one book in this section, Revelation, there are apocalyptic sections and chapters found in other parts of the New Testament (for example, Matthew 23-24). Apocalyptic writing is full of images and visions and is difficult to interpret, but there is a very specific blessing attached to its reading (see Revelation 1:3).

The unity of the Bible

Obviously, a book written by many different authors over more than a thousand years will have great differences and styles of writing. The unity of the Bible doesn't lie in its linguistic style or its genre. Its unity lies in its message. What the Bible teaches about God, his relationship to humanity, the human tendency to go astray from God, and the constant need for God to find, renew and restore persons to himself, is strikingly clear and uniform. The Bible itself makes claims for its unity (see 1 Peter 1:20-21; 1 Corinthians 2:10,13; 2 Timothy 3:16-17). The Scriptures teach that God, by the Holy Spirit, moved the authors to write what they wrote. Sometimes God himself dictated the material (for example, the Ten Commandments in Exodus 20:1-17, and the letters to the seven churches in Revelation 2:1-3:22). Much more frequently, God breathed into the minds of the writers his Word, and they recorded it in their own writing styles. This accounts for the wonderful diversity in the Bible and yet its consistent unity in message and thought.

Is the Bible a completed book?

The Bible is a unique, one-in-the-world book. God is its source, and it is complete. Nothing remains to be added. Since the Bible is God's self-revelation and since in Jesus Christ the full and final disclosure has been made, nothing needs to be added to this revelation (Hebrews 1:1-3). Salvation is complete; victory over death has been accomplished; the curse spoken to Adam and Eve has been reversed; history is progressing toward a final closure.

However, we must be open to new light from the existing Scriptures because the application of God's Word is constantly finding new expressions. In home Bible study groups, in Bible institutes, colleges and seminaries, in Sunday School classes, in churches and in study conferences, God, by the Holy Spirit, opens the Scriptures to us in new and powerful ways. In one sense, every new generation must experience and find God's truth for itself.

Is the Bible trustworthy?

We increasingly hear criticisms that the Bible is merely a human book. The church, however, has affirmed the Bible as God's self-disclosure to the human family. Without the Bible, we would know very little about God, about Jesus Christ and about his plan for humanity. The Scriptures, made clear to us by the Holy Spirit (John 16:5-16), lead us to God and tell us the truth about God.

How can we know with certainty that the Bible is true and can be believed? Here are four reasons:

The witness of the Scriptures themselves. The Scriptures attest that Jesus Christ is God incarnate. Even his enemies acknowledged his authority and were amazed at his teaching. Jesus himself said, "Anyone who has seen me has seen the Father" (John 14:9).

The unity of the message. Usually, if there is a fraudulent story to be circulated, it is difficult to get people to agree on the details of the story. There is, however, in the Bible a remarkable unity concerning the character of God, the nature of humanity, the need for salvation and its provision in Jesus Christ. The apostles, after Pentecost, preached this theme again and again, pointing out the historical continuity between the Old Testament stories and the culminating life and work of Christ (Acts 2, 7). It is, indeed, one story from beginning to end.

The evidence of changed lives. The claim of the Good News, the gospel, is that in Jesus Christ "old things pass away" and people are made into new beings (2 Corinthians 5:17). Peter was transformed from a fearful person into a bold preacher (Acts 2:14ff) and a gracious statesman (Acts 10:1-11:18); Paul was turned from a murderer (Acts 8:1-3) into a witness for Christ before kings and judges (Acts 24:1-27). The story of a changed life has been repeated millions of times throughout the history of the church, as people bear witness to the life-changing power of Christ. The Scriptures must be true because they produce what they claim.

The need for faith. But, when all is said and done, the Bible must still be received as God's Word by faith and not because of logical proof (1 Corinthians 2:14). The greatest assurance of all is the inner witness of the Holy Spirit. Jesus said: "If any person does his [God's] will, he shall know whether the teaching is from God" (John 7:17). Conversely, to the unbelieving Jews, Jesus noted: "He who is of God hears the words of God; the reason why you do not hear them is that you are not of God" (John 8:47).

Helpful suggestions in reading the Bible

To gain maximum benefit from the Scriptures, here are a few suggestions which will help you read the Bible wisely:

In one sense, the Bible must be treated like any other book. In other words, it must be read, and you must understand what it says. Since all of our English Bibles are translations from the Hebrew/Aramaic and Greek versions, choose a translation which is readable. It is wise to read many different translations. Such reading of the Scriptures will give the reader new insights.

The Bible is a very old book. It was written in a time and culture very different from the one in which we live. The more we understand this ancient world, the richer the Scriptures will become to us. Join a Bible study group where you can learn from others' study of the Scriptures. Also, read good, helpful books which will explain the meaning of texts so that you can transfer those meanings to our culture and time.

The Bible is a special book. It is like no other book. The Bible, primarily, is God's self-revelation to humanity. Its message is the power of God for salvation. It is possible to understand what the words say, but to miss entirely the meaning of its message. To understand fully what God is saying to us through his Word, we must allow the Holy Spirit within us to deliver the spiritual meaning to us. To read the Scriptures with benefit, we need to have both the head and heart engaged in the process. Thoughtful and prayerful reading of the Scriptures will make the message of the Bible clear and rich for us. Reading it merely as one would read a novel might give us factual information, but the spiritual dimension of the Scriptures will be missing.

The Bible and obedience. Finally, read with the intent of obeying God's directives. When the Word of God is understood and applied to our lives, it becomes the instrument God uses to bring us to maturity and spiritual well-being. The intent of salvation is not only to give us eternal life, but also to allow us to live well in society as a witness to what God intended for his creation. The most important factor in reading and studying God's Word is the attitude we bring to it. The Scriptures must be read with an open mind, a ready heart and a willing and humble spirit. If we do this, then the Bible will be to us the "Word of his grace which is able to build you up and give you the inheritance among all those who are sanctified" (Acts 20:32).

The need for summary statements

The Scriptures are very old and were written over many centuries. They also were written in many different forms: poetry, histories, genealogies, apocalyptic imagery, prophetic judgement speeches, letters, apologetic and theological reflections, parables and a host of other genres. The Scriptures, written in these various forms address many of the same subjects, but in different ways. A confession of faith, or summary statement, is a short, clear summary of what the Bible teaches on specific topics.

It is important to note that not everything the Bible teaches on a topic can be included in a summary statement. Therefore, the persons writing these summary statements choose what they think are the most important parts of the topic.

Obviously, it is to our advantage to have carefully warded summary statements of the Bible's essential teachings. It is possible for us to gain an understanding of the teaching of the Scriptures quite easily simply by studying these summary statements.

The dangers of summary statements

There are also dangers associated with confessions of faith. We must remember that it is the Scriptures that are the Word of God, while summary statements are the work of human beings. Summary statements are God's word to us only insofar as they accurately reflect the teaching of the Scriptures.

Because summary statements give us an easy way to understand the teachings of Scripture, it is possible to study the summary statements and to have a considerable knowledge of the teachings of the Bible, without ever digging deeply into the Scriptures themselves.

The Mennonite Brethren churches have always emphasized the importance of all Christians reading the Bible and interpreting it, under the guidance of the Holy Spirit, for themselves. However, to guard against the misinterpretation of Scriptures, the church has also insisted that individual interpretations of a text be tested within the church, the community of faith. For this reason, our churches have encouraged regular Sunday school participation from preschool to adult, home and church Bible study groups, and Bible exposition conferences. A strong, spiritual church is a church which knows the Scriptures well.

Furthermore, the Epistle to the Hebrews warns that the church should not be satisfied with only the basics of the faith: "*Therefore, let us move beyond the elementary teachings about Christ and be taken forward to maturity, not laying again the foundation of repentance from acts that lead to death, and of faith in God, instruction about cleansing rites, the laying on of hands, the resurrection of the dead, and eternal judgement.*" (Hebrews 6:1-2) Christian maturity demands that we have a greater understanding of the Scriptures than only "the elementary teachings about Christ". To know God, we need to understand "the full counsel of God" (Acts 20:27), which includes the full range of things about which the Bible speaks. This is a life-long project. The ultimate goal of the church is that each person will "stand firm in all the will of God, mature and fully assured" (Colossians 4:12).

The Mennonite Brethren Confession of Faith

The Mennonite Brethren Church came into being in 1860 in Russia when it separated from the larger Mennonite community over matters of faith and lifestyle. By 1902 it had developed and printed the first uniquely Mennonite Brethren Confession of Faith. This Confession was translated into English in 1940. In 1967 a new Confession of Faith was commissioned – a statement which would address a church now living in North America rather than in Europe. After seven drafts, it was approved in 1975.

In the early 1990s revisions were sought on a number of articles, and with that came a desire to review the wording of the entire Confession. Two new articles were added. The need for these additional articles comes from our interaction with the society in which we live. Technology allows medical practitioners to intervene in the normal life cycle: therefore an article entitled, "The Sanctity of Human Life" states our convictions on this matter. North American society is becoming much more pluralistic: therefore an article entitled "Christianity and Other Faiths" answers the question, "Is Jesus Christ the only way to God?"

NOTES:

NOTES:

chapter three
Living the Christian life

Conversion is only the beginning of a new life within the Kingdom of God, a life with great promise and wonderful possibilities. The Bible uses several metaphors to describe this new life.

First, the Bible uses the metaphor of a child growing from a new-born infant to full maturity (1 Peter 2:1-2) to describe the process of growth which is to be normal in the life of the new believer.

Second, life in the Kingdom of God is like a journey — a journey which will take us to high places from where we can scan the vistas below, but also to depths which will test us and our staying power profoundly. In both good and bad times, we need a maturity which will give us balance (Proverbs 30:89).

Third, when we receive salvation, God declares us to be righteous in his sight. The Christian life is the process by which this righteousness, bit by bit, is implemented into life. In the New Testament, every believer is declared to be a saint (a holy person), and Christian growth is the process whereby we become what God has already declared us to be (Philippians 3:16).

Fourth, the Christian life is the process of developing our relationship with God. It is important that we not only know about God, but that we also know God personally and intimately. To know God, we, like David the Psalmist, need to hunger and thirst for God (Psalm 42:1-2). Jesus said, "Blessed are those who hunger and thirst for righteousness, for they will be filled" (Matthew 5:6).

SIX DISCIPLINES OF THE SPIRITUAL LIFE

Spiritual growth, like all other kinds of personal growth, does not happen unintentionally. Following is a discussion of the principles which lead to spiritual maturity. Most Christians, new and mature, need some structure in order to grow spiritually. However, since there is a very fine line between a structured, ordered life and legalism, which deadens the freedom to which we are called (Galatians 5:1), each person must be on guard so that the spiritual disciplines don't become legalism, a form, trapping the believer in a dead routine.

The discipline of prayer

Prayer is simply speaking to God about the things which are present in our lives and in the lives of those whom we know. The Bible is full of examples of persons who prayed to God. Their prayers included admission of the need for national renewal and repentance (2 Chronicles 7:14; Ezra 9:6-15); requests for God's particular promises to be fulfilled (Daniel 10:1-11:1); cries of the heart to be forgiven (Psalm 51); and cries from the depths of despair (Psalm 88).

Jesus often prayed to his Father. He prayed for God to bless and multiply the five loaves and two fishes (Matthew 14:13-21); he prayed with great intensity in Gethsemane that he would fulfil the purpose for which he had come to earth (Matthew 26:36-46); and he asked God to forgive those who were executing him (Luke 23:34). Sometimes we don't know what he prayed about, but we do know that he spent a night in communion and prayer with his Father (Matthew 14:23).

In the prayer he taught his disciples, commonly known as The Lord's Prayer (Matthew 6:9-13), Jesus gave us a model of the things about which we should pray. The great temptation in prayer is to become too self-centred. Check to see if your prayer life has the following elements: worship, praise and thanks-giving, desire and longing, communion with God, submission, watchfulness, petition (requests) and intercession (requests for other people).

In the prayer which he prayed with the disciples just prior to his trial (John 17), sometimes called The High Priestly Prayer, Jesus focused attention, not on himself, but rather on those who were part of his Kingdom.

In our prayers we pray for those whom we know and for the wider world in which we live including those in authority — prime ministers, presidents and kings — because they, too, are in need of God's wisdom and blessing (1 Timothy 2:1-7).

The discipline of Scripture

The Scriptures are very important in the life of the Christian. There are some things which every human being can know instinctively about God (Romans 1), but there are some important things to know about God which are revealed to us only in the Bible.

The Bible is the record of God's intervention in human affairs; it tells how God, through Christ, has set out to bring salvation to humanity. It also gives instruction on how to live within the Kingdom of God. It isn't enough to read and know the Bible; the Bible must also affect the way the Christian lives. Someone has said: "If the proof of the pudding is in the eating, then the proof of Christianity lies in the life of its adherents".

The Word of God is described as the source of life (John 6:68), as spiritual food which neutralizes the impulses to sin (1 Peter 2:1-2), as the means to develop spiritual understanding (1 Corinthians 2:13-14), as light to guide us through the maze of life's problems (Psalm 119:105; John 17:17) and as truth to lead us faithfully to God, who is ultimate Truth (John 1:14, 17;8:32; 16:13).

The promise of a rich and abundant life is given to those who study and obey the teachings of the Word of God (Psalm 1:1-6; Joshua 1:8; Psalm 119:1-8).

A maturing Christian will read the Bible regularly so that its words and teaching become an integral part of life. The Scriptures themselves encourage the hiding of God's Word in our hearts as a buffer against the temptation to fall into sin (Psalm 119:11). A good way to do this is to memorize favourite verses or passages of Scripture.

The discipline of fellowship and worship

Through the new birth, the believer becomes a member of God's family (Galatians 3:26). This family gathers regularly for a variety of purposes.

The first-century church gathered on the first day of the week, Sunday, to celebrate the resurrection (Acts 20:7; 1 Corinthians 16:2). In this gathering, two specific things happened. The first was the strengthening of the believer and the church body. The church gathered to build one another up and to become one, so that a strong, unified witness to God's redeeming grace can be maintained (1 Corinthians 12:1-14). The church gathered as a unified body to become equipped to do the work of ministry (Ephesians 4:1-16).

The second reason to gather was to worship, to give glory, honour and praise to God. God's people have always been ready to sing and speak praises to God for his mighty deeds (Exodus 15:1-18; Psalm 145:1-7; Acts 2:14-41). The New Testament church celebrated the atoning work of Christ through the Lord's Supper (Acts 2:42). It was also encouraged to sing, speak, make music and give thanks to God (Ephesians 5:15-20).

The New Testament also adds a very important component to worship which was not present in the Old Testament. Worship must be more than words. Worship is tied to service (Romans 12:1-2); that is, God is worshipped when we serve him.

It is important for every Christian to be part of a local congregation. We are counselled by the Scriptures "not to forsake the gathering together of God's people" (Hebrews 10:25), and to offer, through Jesus, a continual sacrifice of praise (Hebrews 13:15).

The discipline of money

The Bible has much to say about possessions. This shouldn't surprise us because so much of life is comprised of earning a living. Since we live in a world where security is a very fragile matter, we tend to want to create security by accumulating possessions.

Money and possessions can be either a blessing or curse. We are instructed to pray for "our daily bread" (Matthew 6:11) and are assured of our Father's care (Matthew 6:25-34); but we are also repeatedly warned about the insidious, corrupting nature of possessions. The Rich Fool (Luke 12:13-21) lost everything in his pursuit of material possessions, and the Rich Ruler (Luke 18:18-30) missed the gate which leads to eternal life because he couldn't give up his riches. We are warned not to accumulate riches which are temporary (Matthew 6:19-24) but to deposit riches in heaven where they will be secure. We are warned not to love money, but to be rich in contentment (Hebrews 13:5), and to place our hope in God, not wealth (1 Timothy 6:6-10, 17).

The Christian is called a steward (Matthew 25:14-30); that is, possessions are not to be owned; they are to be managed in a responsible manner. Faithful stewardship helps the Christian overcome the dangers of riches and avoid selfishness (1 Timothy 6:6-10). Giving is to be according to income (1 Corinthians 16:2), and God's blessing rests on those practicing faithful stewardship (2 Corinthians 8:2; Acts 20:35; Malachi 3:10; Luke 6:38).

The discipline of time

The Psalmist suggests that "the length of our days is seventy years — or eighty, if we have the strength", and then goes on to urge the good use of time because it is short and each moment is precious (Psalm 90:10, 12).

The New Testament echoes this sentiment. It warns us to be careful how we live because the days are short and the times are evil (Ephesians 5:16-17). It encourages us to live each moment of life in a worthy manner (Colossians 3:17), and discourages the wasting of time through idleness (1 Thessalonians 5:14). When time is not disciplined, it tends to be wasted.

Some churches ask for "a tithe of time" from their members; that is, they ask all their members to devote at least 10% of their time to the work and ministry of the church. The church is given spiritual gifts by God, but these gifts come to the church in the form of people. It takes time to practice the gifts and to build up the church body (1 Corinthians 12:14).

The discipline of accountability

The Bible asserts that we are interdependent and need one another (1 Corinthians 12:12-27). It also notes that when one part suffers and is hurt, the whole body suffers and is hurt (1 Corinthians 12:26).

Often, the subject of accountability is raised within the context of church discipline. Church discipline is certainly one area of accountability, but accountability is much broader than that. Accountability is living our lives openly before both the Christian community and the watching world.

The members of Christ's body are accountable both to God and to the local church. One way to be accountable is to be part of a small group. In this group, both young and mature Christians can share their joys and sorrows, their victories and defeats, and hear the counsel, correction, affirmation and teaching of other Christians. As we submit to one another, God continues to work out his will in us.

THE IMPORTANCE OF PERSONAL INTEGRITY

The person who professes to be a Christian should live like one. The best argument for the reality of the gospel is a consistent Christian lifestyle. On the other hand, inconsistency in the way a person lives destroys the power of Christian witness. The call of Christ to his followers was to live with openness; to allow the light of our life to be seen; and to be the salt of the earth (Matthew 5:13-16).

Salvation opens the door to discipleship. Discipleship means "to follow in the way of Jesus". In other words, the Christian is a person who patterns his or her lifestyle after the life of Jesus. Personal integrity means that the Christian absorbs the teachings of Jesus Christ and lives them out in a consistent, God-honouring way. Outlined below are five important areas where this should be done.

Discipleship and ethics

"In Jesus Christ", writes John H. Redekop, "salvation and ethics come together." Another way of saying this is that when salvation comes to us, a new life with new ideals and standards has awakened within each of us. To be a disciple means to discipline ourselves to follow the standards of God as set out in the Bible (Ephesians 4:21-32). "Ethics" is the word we use to describe human conduct in terms of right and wrong.

To live godly, upright lives is not an easy thing. The issue isn't so much that we have trouble discerning what is right and what is wrong; rather, the problem is that we often don't have the strength, resources, or will to conquer our sinful impulses.

Every Christian, to some degree, is a walking civil war. The old nature, which is still alive within us, is in conflict with the new nature, which we received from Christ at conversion (Galatians 5:13-26). Sometimes we do the things we don't want to do; and sometimes the things which we want to do, evade us (Romans 7:18-27). Sometimes the fruit of Spirit is evident in our lives (Galatians 5:22-23); at other times, the works of our sinful nature are expressed (Galatians 5:19-21).

It is for this reason that the church has often been accused, by those who are not a part of it, of being-full of hypocrites. In one sense, this is true. We are sinners saved by grace, and because we are sinners, sin will sometimes be evident in our lives and in the corporate life of the church.

Although this is the reality, it need not be that way. Nor should it be that way. Peter encourages us to grow into maturity (2 Peter 3:18), and this is done by heeding his instruction:

"Dear friends, I urge you, as foreigners and exiles, to abstain from sinful desires, which war against your soul. Live such good lives among the pagans that, though they accuse you of doing wrong, they may see your good deeds and glorify God on the day he visits us" (1 Peter 2:11-12).

Paul admonishes us to walk a life worthy of the gospel and of Christ (Ephesians 4:1-3); James begs us to live by the wisdom that is from above, not the wisdom of this world (James 3:13-18); and the writer of the Epistle to the Hebrews warns against intentional sinning after receiving the gift of salvation (Hebrews 10:26-27).

Discipleship and speech

Jesus warned that our tongue will betray us (Matthew 15:16-20; Mark 7:20-23). James warns us not to speak too rashly (James 1:19-20); to remember that good deeds are much better than good talk (1:26-27); to recognize that the tongue is so powerful it can set a forest ablaze, or, like a small rudder, steer a huge ship (3:3-6); and to beware that out of the same mouth, as strange as this may appear, can come blessing and cursing (3:9-10). His final injunction, "Brothers and sisters, this ought not to be" (3:10b), is a powerful word of caution about the devastating power of the tongue.

The Book of Proverbs is filled with pithy sayings warning about the power of words. Life and death are in the words we speak (18:21); we can wound with words (12:18); we can build up and heal with words (12:25; 16:24); and we can ruin persons through flattery (29:5). In a telling bit of poetry, the writer of Proverbs argues that of the seven things which God detests, three have to do with our speech: a lying tongue, a false witness and creating dissension in the community of faith (Proverbs 6:16-19).

Gossip is one of the deadly sins in society. Gossip is idle, malicious talk. It is talk which destroys a person's reputation. It is particularly insidious because it is practiced behind closed doors and in whispered voices. Gossip is listed in the catalogue of sins over which God will pass judgement (Romans 1:28-31). Gossip is listed in the same breath with quarrelling, anger, arrogance and sexual immorality (2 Corinthians 12:19-21). Paul says: *"Let your conversation always be full of grace, seasoned with salt, so that you may know how to answer everyone"* (Colossians 4:6).

Discipleship and interpersonal relationships

Integrity in the Christian life is most noticeable in interpersonal relationships. The new birth gives the believer entry into the family of God, which is to be characterized by love and care. Repeatedly, Christians are called to "love one another" (John 15:17; 1 John 3:11; 3:18; 4:7-21).

The Bible teaches that there is a strong connection between loving God and loving our fellow human being. Jesus commended the lawyer for his understanding that the commands to love God and neighbour are the greatest commands of God (Leviticus 19:18; Mark 12:28-34). The Scriptures further state that every human relationship is to be infused with Christian understanding.

Marriage. Marriage is the primary, intimate relationship of adulthood. Marriage dates back to the creation of humanity, when God created man and woman in his own image (Genesis 5:1-2). The attraction of male to female, and female to male, is natural, and, by God's design, man and woman are intended to be united in covenant (Genesis 2:18-25). (However, a person who remains single, because of personal choice or for other reasons, is not inferior to the married person in any way.)

Marriage is to be characterized by love and care and is to be for all of life (Ephesians 5:21-33). Divorce (and remarriage) are not the Christian ideal (Matthew 19:3-9). The Scriptures make it clear that the partners in marriage ought to agree on matters of faith and that a believer ought not to marry an unbeliever (2 Corinthians 6:14).

Sexual relations are not to be practiced outside of marriage, either before marriage or with partners other than husband or wife. Adultery is a serious sin in that it breaks trust and destroys the intimacy which is part of the marriage union (Ephesians 5:3). The biblical view of marriage is so high that sexual sin is presented in the darkest colors. Sexual sin is an exchange of true intimacy for an imitation (Proverbs 5:19-20), a parting with one's honour (Proverbs 5:9) and a throwing away of that which is dearest in life (Proverbs 29:3; 6:26).

The divine arrangement that the husband be the head of wife is much more a matter of responsibility than of privilege (Ephesians 5:23). The husband is to love his wife as Christ loves the church: realistically, loyally, purposefully, wilfully and absolutely (Ephesians 5:21-33). The wife is to respond to such love willingly and openly.

Parents and children. Children are a gift from God. Happy is the family which has them (Psalm 127:5). Parents are to guide in a loving, wise manner while children are too young and inexperienced to make discriminating choices (Ephesians 6:4; Colossians 3:21). Parents are to instruct children in the ways of God (Deuteronomy 6:4-9) and to discipline them to live useful, godly lives (Proverbs 1:8-9). Parents, particularly fathers, are not to exasperate and badger children but are to bring them up in the training and instruction of the Lord (Ephesians 6:4).

Children are to respect, honor and obey their parents (Colossians 3:20; Ephesians 6:1-3). A long and good life is promised to those who do (Ephesians 6:1-3; Deuteronomy 5:16).

Employers and employees. The New Testament was written during a time when Rome ruled much of Europe and the Ancient Near East. Slavery was accepted as a part of that world. At its zenith, the Roman Empire had approximately sixty million slaves.

The gospel was preached into this culture declaring that in Christ all barriers had come down (Galatians 3:26-29). In the church, there was to be no distinction between Gentile and Jew, slave and free, male and female.

To make a connection between master and slave, about which the New Testament speaks (Ephesians 6:5-9; Colossians 3:22-4:1), and modem labour agreements is difficult. There are, however, principles which apply to employers and employees. Employers are to be reasonable and just, remembering that they, too, are under God (Colossians 4:1). Employees are to be responsive to their employers and do their work well. They are to do this, not for praise, but because of reverence for God (Colossians 3:22-25).

In other words, the Bible teaches that both employer and employee are under the careful watch of God. Both are to be respectful, to be courteous and to live worthy of their calling (Philippians 2:15; I Peter 2:17), all the while understanding that in the church there is no distinction between employer and employee.

Peace: The way of Christ

At the heart of the gospel is the message of peace. Jesus came to address the enmity and gulf that separates humanity from God. In Christ, peace replaces this enmity. Paul asserts that Christ "is our peace" (Ephesians 2:15) and that the mission of Christ on earth was "to preach peace to those far away and to those nearby" (Ephesians 2:17 NIV). Again and again, the letters of the New Testament are opened with the distinctly Christian greeting: "Grace and peace to you" (Romans 1:7; 1 Corinthians 1:3; 2 Corinthians 1:2; etc.).

Jesus himself taught that the way of peace lies in extending forgiveness (Matthew 6:14-15; Matthew 18:21-35), in blessing our enemies rather than cursing them (Matthew 5:43-48) and in binding up the wounds of those who are different from us (Luke 10:25-37).

Peace must become a way of life for the mature Christian. Too often this has been interpreted too narrowly, as if it only applies to times of warfare and is a prohibition against killing. It is that, to be sure, but it is more. Peace is not only the absence of hostility; it is putting in place things which create wholeness and wellbeing. To follow Jesus means that we help those in need (Matthew 25:31-46).

The Christian and the State

Human government was instituted by God (Romans 13:1-7) and given the responsibility to maintain an orderly society for the common good of the citizens. Christians are commanded to be subject to government and to pay proper respect to civil authorities.

Christians, like all other citizens, pay taxes and customs (1 Peter 2:17; Matthew 22:24). Furthermore, Christians are to be a model of good behaviour by being obedient, by being ready to do good, by living peacefully, by being considerate of every person and by showing humility — a humility which will not allow anyone to be slandered (Titus 3:1-2).

The Scriptures call on believers to pray regularly and fervently for those in authority (2 Timothy 2:1-2; Jeremiah 29:7) and, insofar as is possible, to submit to every authority "for the Lord's sake" (1 Peter 2:13).

Each believer is a citizen of two kingdoms: the Kingdom of God and the earthly nation where he or she lives. By virtue of being members of God's Kingdom, we become exemplary citizens in our earthly kingdoms. However, when a government makes demands upon Christians which are in clear violation of the will of God, then each believer must choose to obey God rather than human government (Acts 5:29).

In times of civil disturbances and war, Christians are faced with the question of whether to take part in acts of violence, even to the extent of taking human life. Here the teaching of the New Testament is clear. Human life is sacred; Christians should not kill (Matthew 5:21-22; 26:52).

In cases of personal loss, Christians should not seek revenge or use force to get restitution (Romans 12:19; 1 Peter 2:21-23; 3:9; Matthew 5: 38-42). In the event of war, a believer should not take up arms or be trained in the use of them. Our warfare and weapons are spiritual (2 Corinthians 10:3-4).

Having said this, it is also important to call all Christians to be involved in their communities for the good of society. Social and economic improvements are good and desirable, and Christians should be ready to support all initiatives which enhance the well-being of all persons, particularly those who can't help themselves.

A LIFE OF SERVICE

The Christian is called to a life of service. The New Testament knows nothing of a private, self-centered faith which participates only in the benefits which have come to the believer in Jesus Christ. While it is true that being a Christian gives the believer some wonderful benefits, there are also some responsibilities which go along with the benefits. When we are born into the family of God, we accept responsibility for serving faithfully within this new family.

Jesus was very clear that faithfulness in service is the measure of success in the church (Matthew 25:14-30). Faithfulness is not determined so much by the volume of return, but rather by the faithfulness of the person in using the talents/gifts that have been given by God. What is unacceptable is returning our gifts and talents to God unused.

Paul repeatedly counselled the church to be active in service (Romans 12:11). He spoke of himself as a *"slave of Jesus Christ"* (Romans 1:1). James, the physical brother of Jesus (that is, they had the same mother, Mary), opens his short letter with the same words. The word Paul and James use to describe themselves is doulos. This common first-century word, which our English translations usually render as *"servant"*, is the Greek word for slave. Doulos is a very strong word. It describes those who have no rights except to serve the will of their Master. Of course, the difference between a slave in the Roman Empire and *"a slave of Jesus Christ"* is that the former is a slave against his will while the latter is a slave by an act of the will.

Spiritual gifts

The Bible teaches that each person is given gifts for service and ministry by the Holy Spirit. Listed below are some important points concerning the Christian and the gifts of the Spirit.

Each believing person has received a gift/gifts for service. The New Testament assures us that each believer has been given "a gift/gifts of grace" by the Holy Spirit (1 Corinthians 12:7). These gifts are given "just as he (the Holy Spirit) determines" (1 Corinthians 12:11) and are given for the common good of the church (1 Corinthians 12:7). Furthermore, these gifts are inter-dependent, part of a grand scheme in which each person supplies what the other parts of the body need for a healthy existence (1 Corinthians 12:12-26). The gifts are to be exercised with love (1 Corinthians 13:1-13).

Many gifts are available to the members of the body. Three New Testament texts give lists of spiritual gifts:

1 Corinthians 12	Ephesians 4	Romans 12
Word of wisdom	Apostleship	Prophesy
Word of knowledge	Prophesy	Helps
Faith	Evangelism	Teaching
Healing	Pastoring	Exhorting
Miracles	Teaching	Giving
Prophesy		Prophecy
Discernment		Administration
Tongues		Showing mercy
Interpretation of tongues		
Apostleship		
Teaching		
Helps		
Administration		

There are other gifts noted in the New Testament: Paul had the gift of celibacy (1 Corinthians 7:1-7); Barnabas had the gift of encouragement (Acts 4:36). These lists are not intended to be exhaustive, but they give a good picture of what is necessary in order for the church to do the work of ministry.

Often it is assumed that the more public gifts (such as preaching, teaching and administration) are the more important gifts. While they are important, it is the less public gifts which help the body reach maturity. We do well, once again, to remind ourselves that the measure of success in the Kingdom of God is not the volume or visibility of our gifts; rather, it is our faithfulness in using the gifts that have been given. When all the gifts are present in the body and each believing person faithfully uses his or her gifts, the church will function smoothly. It will be able to build itself up and to minister to one another and to the unbelieving society around it.

Finding and developing your gift/s

For new Christians, probably the most vexing thing about the gifts of the Spirit is trying to discern which gifts the Spirit has given to them. Here are a few practical suggestions to help in the discernment process.

Begin with your special interests. The most obvious place to begin is with those things which are your special interest. Each person is born with certain talents and abilities. There is frequently a strong correlation between our talents and the gifts of the Spirit. This relationship ought to be explored thoroughly.

Test your gifts by trial and error. As strange as it might sound, you ought to be adventuresome in your exploration of the gifts of the Spirit. Try them out. You will never know what you can do if you don't experiment. Jesus roundly scolded the person with one talent (Matthew 25:24-27) because all he could think to do was bury his talent in the ground.

Some gifts come through experience. For example, God often uses a particularly difficult experience to make us sensitive to others in the same plight and to come alongside with a gentle touch and word of encouragement.

Some gifts are more learned than granted. Some gifts are learned through "*doing*". Those with the gift of teaching or the gift of leading music and worship have enhanced those gifts through training and practice. Sometimes we are inclined to think that if something doesn't come easily to us, we don't have a gift in that area. Gifts are never given to us in their full-blown maturity. We grow into them. Paul also suggests that it is permissible to "eagerly desire" greater gifts.

Attitude is very important. Our attitudes are important. All believers ought to give the best they are capable of in service of God and the body of Christ. Instead, sometimes we give to the body of Christ that which is left over, after the busy day of work is finished.

God will bless the work of the person whose attitude is right. Some persons are very talented, but they don't bless the body because there is a self-serving tone in their service; they want to be the "star of the show". Others, who may not be as talented, bless the body richly because they are aware that this is their service to Christ. God does not easily share his glory with others (Isaiah 42:8; 48:11) and therefore does not bless those who serve for their own interests.

Discuss your gifts and their development with a leader in the church. There is much help available to you in the church. Talk to someone about your interests and emerging gifts. Ask for opportunities to test them. Ask to be placed in a mentoring relationship with someone able to give guidance. Pray about your service opportunities, and keep an eye open for places where you can serve God and the body.

Furthermore, many gifts are given by God to reach into the lives of those who are outside of the body of Christ. Gifts such as helping, showing mercy and evangelism are richly used by God to help open the door to salvation.

A LIFE OF WITNESS

The Christian is also called to live a life of witness. It is useful, at the outset to make a distinction between a life of witness and the gift of evangelism. By "**witness**", we mean confessing publicly that Jesus is our Saviour and Lord. By "*the gift of evangelism*", we mean that special gift of the Holy Spirit which enables some individuals to be particularly convincing in bringing many people to the place where they will receive God's wonderful gift of forgiveness. Every Christian is to be a witness to the grace of God, but not every Christian has the gift of evangelism.

Every Christian is called to be a witness. Jesus told his followers that "*whoever publicly acknowledges me, I will also acknowledge before my Father in heaven. But whoever publicly disowns me, I will disown before my Father in heaven*" (Matthew 10:32-33). Paul links making a confession of the lordship of Christ to salvation (Romans 10:8-10), and Peter exhorts us to be ready to give reason for the hope we have in Christ (1 Peter 3:15).

Overcoming fear

Fear is very debilitating. Many Christians, both new and mature, live godly personal lives but are filled with fear and do not readily share a word of witness with their friends and neighbours. Fear keeps them from talking about their faith. Most are afraid because they think they will have to answer some difficult theological question. Rather than risking failure, they tend to be quiet. Others are so afraid to say something publicly that they will even put off being baptized because they can't bear standing before a group of people to share their faith-story. Listed below are some pointers for bearing witness to the new life which we have received in Christ.

Start with something simple. Preparation is helpful to giving a word of witness. Speaking of your faith is simply telling what has happened to you. A Christian is a person who has a personal relationship with God through the forgiveness of sins. If you are afraid to speak, start by rehearsing your own personal faith-story. To be prepared in advance often makes it easier to speak when the time comes.

Don't think you have to preach! Sometimes, Christian people are silent simply because they *"aren't good with words"*. To confess Christ means that we acknowledge that we are believers in Christ Jesus. It isn't preaching a sermon or giving a full defence for our faith; it is simply acknowledging that we are Christians.

It gets easier as you do it regularly. As with other new ventures, it takes time and practice to get good at something. The first time might be awkward and uncomfortable, but through time it becomes easier. Paul knew his faith-story so well that he could tell it virtually the same way again and again (Acts 22:1-21; 26:1-23).

Pray about it. It helps to ask God for courage and strength to bear witness to our faith. God has promised to be with us from the point of our belief to the end of the age (Matthew 28:20). The Holy Spirit lives in us, and Jesus promised his help in a time of crisis (Luke 12:11-12)

Read and make use of good materials. There are many good books to help us develop a strong witness. There are also easy-to-understand "salvation plans" (such as, *Four Spiritual Laws* and *Steps to Peace with God*) which can help us answer questions which might arise in a conversation.

The positive influence of a good life. While the New Testament calls every believer to confess with the tongue that Jesus is Lord (Romans 10:8-10), we ought not to underestimate the powerful witness of a quiet, good, godly life. Ultimately, the proof of our conversion is that we practice a lifestyle which is truly transformed by Christ.

The gospel: In word and deed

The mission of church embraces both evangelism and social action and refuses to let them become divorced from one another. Jesus called his followers to preach the Good News (Matthew 28:18-20), and he called his followers to live with great compassion (Luke 10:36-37). Sadly, modern Christianity has often driven a wedge between these two. Rather than bringing together God's concern for the salvation of every person and God's concern for the plight of the disadvantaged, it seems that the church is ready to argue over which is more important.

Evangelism and social concern belong together. We ought not to do one without the other. The church ought not to hinder one while highlighting the other. God cares deeply for the salvation of each person, and God cares deeply for the plight of the poor, the widowed, the powerless and the disenfranchised.

Menno Simons, one of the founders of the Anabaptist movement, instructed the church with these words:

> "True evangelical faith cannot lie sleeping
>
> for it clothes the naked,
>
> it comforts the sorrowful,
>
> it gives to the hungry food,
>
> and it shelters the destitute."

NOTES:

chapter four
Living in the church, the community of faith

In salvation, the sin that has separated a person from God has been removed. This act of salvation is so important that we tend to ignore other important matters which flow from this act. One such matter is that through salvation we have become part of the people of God.

Describing the community of faith

The Bible uses more than 20 metaphors to describe the community into which each believing person is incorporated. Some are outlined below.

The church. A common biblical word used to describe the people of God is the Greek word ecclesia (often translated "the church"), which means the group of "called-out ones". In the ancient Greek world, this was the common word to describe any group which was called together for a specific purpose. In the New Testament, it is applied to those persons who have been "called out" to become part of the people of God, a community of faith joined together by a covenant made with God and with each other.

Ecclesia is not an accident. The church is the intentional creation of God, through Christ, and we have his word that not even the "gates of hell" can destroy it (Matthew 16:18). The church is the strategic community through which the gospel is spread in the world. The church, as the community of redeemed persons, is also the embodiment of the gospel.

The Kingdom of God. Jesus came preaching the Kingdom of God (Mark 1:14-15). He understood himself to be the King of this Kingdom. He came calling people — men and women, Jews and Gentiles, the rich and the poor, the educated and the barbarians — to come into the Kingdom (Luke 14:15-24).

The Kingdom of God is not a material kingdom comprised of land and wealth; rather, it is a kingdom made up of people who are followers of Jesus Christ. It is comprised of those of every nation who have accepted the reign of God within their own personal lives (1 Corinthians 12:13). In the great worship scene in Revelation 7:9-17, an enormous crowd surrounds God's throne, composed of people "from every race, tribe, nation and language". God's ultimate triumph, in Christ, is to call a people out of darkness and bring them into the Kingdom of light (Colossians 1:13-14). God's mission, in Christ, is to bring together a people from the vast reaches of the earth (Ephesians 3:10-15). God's agent in this mission is the unified, diverse people who are already part of that Kingdom (Ephesians 3:14-21).

The body of Christ (1 Corinthians 12:12-30). The people of God are also called "the body of Christ". The focus of this metaphor is "authority". A body is a unified entity working together in harmony, an integrated system in which each part performs its designated function. A healthy body cannot war within itself; it works as a single unit to accomplish its goal.

Christ is the head of the body. This means at least two things. First, it means that he is in authority over the church. There can be no other; it is Christ who gives direction to his body; it is Christ who calls on each part of the body to do its function so that the goal of being the body can be accomplished.

Second, not only is Christ the head of the body, the church, but he is also the head over all of creation. There is nothing in the world which does not fall under his authority (Ephesians 1:22; Colossians 1:15-20). For the Christian, this means that Christ's headship is far beyond the reach of competing interests; his authority and power are unchallenged; his direction and call for unified action is legitimate and clear. Being a Christian, therefore, means that we belong to Christ. It means that we are called to fit into his scheme of things.

The bride of Christ (Ephesians 5:25-33; 1 Corinthians 13). This metaphor focuses on "love". Christ loves the church the way a bridegroom loves a bride. This means that Christ is for us, with us and beside us. We are the sole object of his love and care. His love is never coercive; it is gentle and kind; it protects and trusts; it is not rude or self-seeking; nor is it consumed by anger (1 Corinthians 13).

Secondly, Christ's intent is for the church to be a growing, beautiful bride, holy, radiant, without spot or wrinkle. He does not stand in the way of her growth and maturity, but encourages it.

The family of God (Ephesians 2:19-22; 1 Peter 2:4-8). The key concept in this metaphor is "belonging". It has both an animate and inanimate component to it. In Ephesians, we are said to be part of "the household of God", which literally means that we are part of God's family. In 1 Peter, we are said to be "living stones" which are being incorporated into the spiritual house which is being built. In other words, we are both the occupants of a house and the house itself. We are both God's family and God's showpiece. We are both the recipients of the message and the visible result of the message.

To belong to the family of God gives us security. We are not part of a family which disowns its children; we are not part of a dysfunctional family in which one person exploits the vulnerability of another; we are not part of a family in which our failures loosen our connectedness with one another. We are a covenant family; we belong together; we are secure.

The Purpose of the church

David Watson tells of seeing a placard carried by a member of the "Jesus People" movement which proclaimed: "Jesus — Yes! Church — No!" There is a lingering feeling that the church sometimes gets in the way of what it is that God wants to do in society, and that a new Christian might be better off not being part of the church.

While it is true that the church frequently does not live up to its ideal, it nonetheless is both the embodiment of the Good News and the agent of the Good News. In the New Testament, the identity of the church and purpose of the church are tied closely together. In other words, what the church is is intimately related to what the church is to do. Peter ties these two together in a dramatic manner (1 Peter 2:9-10).

The identity of the church: Christ's unique possession. 1 Peter 2:9 reads: *"But you are a chosen people, a royal priesthood, a holy nation, God's special possession ...."* To be "chosen" means that God has exercised his will in the establishment of the church; there is nothing random, or accidental, in the establishment of the church and in its continuing life.

To be "royal" means that we have been given a special status by God; "priesthood" implies that we have access to God and have been made a bridge between God and humanity (2 Corinthians 5:11-21).

To be "a holy nation" means that we are part of a new society which embraces all races, all nations, all ethnic distinctives. In this nation, all the barriers which create divisions within the human family, have been torn down. The adjective "holy" means to be different. The people of God are different from all other nations, in the sense that those things that cause divisions and wars in the world, do not cause divisions in the Kingdom of God.

The final phrase "a people belonging to God" defines both the origin of the church and the end of the church. The church belongs to God because it has been created in Christ, and the church's end is in the hands of God, because he possesses and lives in it.

The mission/purpose of the church: To embody this identity through bold living. The 1 Peter 2 text concludes with a strong mission statement: *"that you may declare the praises of him who called you out of darkness into his wonderful light."*

The purpose of the church is to declare the Good News to the world. The church does this in two ways: by its identity (that is, by what it is) and by its proclamation (that is, by what it says). The Good News which is proclaimed is illustrated and demonstrated by the experience of the church. The body of

Christ is comprised of those who once were part of the fractured, broken world of humanity but who have been made whole in Jesus Christ. The proclamation of the church is that this same healing can happen to those who have not yet experienced it.

Why be part of a local church?

Sometimes we hear people say that they are part of the "invisible" body of Christ, the eternal, redeemed family of God which is as old as the human race itself. This is true. Nonetheless, to say that we are part of the body of Christ without also being a part of a local church, the visible body of Christ, is to be in error. When we are born into the family of God, we become part of the people of God which finds its expression in the local church.

The local church is not exclusively the people of God, but it is part of the people of God. The local church, with all of its strengths and weaknesses, is the body of Christ, the bride of Christ and the family of God. There is no other place where these important metaphors find their fulfillment. It is the local church which is the embodiment of the gospel, the agent for God's Good News to be proclaimed, the visible sign that the Kingdom of God is present in the world. It is in the local church that the love of Christ is extended to each person. It is through the local church that "reckless, senseless, random acts of kindness" are done.

To be born again is to be born into a family which has a local flavor and identity. The church, which often tends to hide behind an institutional framework, is really a living organism: It lives, it acts, it grows, it works, it weeps, it laughs, it advances, it retreats. It is not a club, nor is it an organization; it is the living body of Christ.

Discipline in the church

Discipline in the church is discussed in the Bible. In fact, Jesus himself gave us the model for confronting sin in the church (Matthew 18:15-19). When a believing person falls into sin, this person is to be restored gently through warning (Galatians 6:1-2). If confession is made, the assertion that sins will be forgiven (1 John 1:9) then comes into effect. In extreme cases, if the person refuses to repent, that person is to be separated from the believing community (1 Corinthians 5:1-12).

Giving and receiving in the church

The church has much to give to Christians entering it. The Scriptures list at least seven things which the church is to provide for each member. It is:

• to teach (Ephesians 4:11-16);

• to encourage (Hebrews 10:23-25);

• to give guidance and direction (Acts 20:28-35);

• to disciple, or discipline (Matthew 18:15-20);

• to provide fellowship and caring (Acts 2:42);

• to give assistance in time of physical need (Acts 6:1-7; 11:27-30);

• and to provide opportunities for service (Acts 13:1-3; 1 Corinthians 12:1-11).

Christians, in turn, are to give back to the church the things which help others to mature:

• a basic, strong commitment to live and work within the church so that the church is prospered by their gifts (1 Corinthians 12-14);

• prayer (James 5:16; Ephesians 6:18; Philippians 1:4,9);

• fellowship and encouragement to others (Hebrews 10:25);

• stewardship of talents (Romans 12:1-2), time (Ephesians 5:14-16), money (2 Corinthians 8:5; 9:7), influence (2 Corinthians 2:14) and the gospel (1 Corinthians 4:1);

• a Christian lifestyle (Ephesians 5:18; 1 Thessalonians 5:17; 1 Peter 2:2; Philippians 4:8-9; Galatians 5:16; Hebrews 12:1-2);

• a life of service (1 Corinthians 12; Romans 12; 1 Peter 4:10-11);

• and loyalty and a constructive attitude (Matthew 5:23-24; 18:15-17; John 15:12).

EXPRESSING THE COVENANT COMMUNITY: BAPTISM

The Mennonite Brethren Church understands the Scriptures to teach that there are two "ordinances", or symbolic acts, which Christ commanded his followers to keep: baptism and the Lord's Supper. The Mennonite Brethren Church has reached and maintained consensus on the subject of baptism for More than a century. This consensus has been arrived at by studying the Scriptures together. It is expressed in Article 8 of the Mennonite Brethren Confession of Faith:

Confession

We believe that when people receive God's gift of salvation, they are to be baptized in the name of the Father, Son and Holy Spirit. Baptism is a sign of having been cleansed from sin. It is a covenant with the church to walk in the way of Christ through the power of the Spirit.

Meaning

Baptism by water is a public sign that a person has repented of sins, received forgiveness of sins, died with Christ to sin, been raised to newness of life and received the Holy Spirit. Baptism is a sign of the believer's incorporation into the body of Christ as expressed in the local church. Baptism is also a pledge to serve Christ according to the gifts given to each person.

Eligibility

Baptism is for those who confess Jesus Christ as Lord and Savior and commit themselves to follow Christ in obedience as members of the local church. Baptism is for those who understand its meaning, are able to be accountable to Christ and the church, and voluntarily request it on the basis of their faith response to Jesus Christ.

Practice

We practice water baptism by immersion administered by the local church. Local congregations may receive into membership those who have been baptized by another mode on their confession of faith. Persons who claim baptism as infants and wish to become members of a Mennonite Brethren congregation are to receive baptism on their confession of faith.

The meaning of the word "baptize"

The verb "to baptize" in Greek means "to dip, to plunge, to immerse". It was a secular word with a much broader definition and application than only the religious one. It was a word which had a specific literal meaning, but was also used in a metaphorical and symbolic way.

The literal meaning. "To baptize" was used to describe both "dipping" in general and the more specific act of plunging something into a substance to change its character. For example, it was used by the blacksmith who plunged red-hot iron into water to temper, or harden, it. It was also used by the dealer who would plunge linen cloth into dye to change its color.

The metaphorical meaning. Jesus, when speaking to the disciples about the agony of his coming death, used the word "baptize" in a metaphorical sense: "I have a baptism to undergo, and how distressed I am until it is completed!" (Luke 12:50). The word was also used metaphorically to describe how Christ plunges the new believer into the Holy Spirit to change his or her character (Mark 1:8; John 1:33). This is another way to speak of salvation.

The symbolic meaning. Baptism, as it is practiced in the New Testament is both a literal and a symbolic act. In Romans 6:3-7 we are informed that we have been "baptized into Christ Jesus" and "into his death". The literal part of this baptism is the water into which we are plunged; the symbolic part of this baptism is that we are baptized into Christ Jesus and into his death.

A sign of incorporation into the church

In the ancient world, baptism was used as a sign of initiation into many different interest groups, as a sign- that the person baptized was accepting a new set of values, a new way of life. It was used in this way by John the Baptizer, who called on the Jewish people to repent and to be part of a new righteousness different from the existing form of religion (Mark 1:1-5; Matthew 3:1-10).

The early church quite readily accepted this common form of incorporation when it began using water baptism. Jesus, in his final charge to his disciples, instructed them "to go and make disciples of all nations, baptizing them ..." (Matthew 28:20). Through baptism, believers are incorporated into the church. Baptism is not a means of grace; rather, it symbolically illustrates that grace, through faith, has come. Baptism is usually a one-time experience and marks the beginning of life within the Kingdom of God. It is an act of initiation into the covenant community which is the body of Christ.

Salvation and baptism linked. In New Testament times, salvation and baptism were very closely linked. Again and again we read "believed-and-were-baptized" language (Acts 2:40-41; 8:36-40; 10:48; 16:15; 16:33). These two events, conversion and baptism, were seen as two sides of the same experience. In salvation the gulf separating God and humanity was bridged, and in baptism this reality was symbolically revealed to the watching world, announcing that a new set of values, a new life had begun. Baptism was understood to fulfill, in part, the command of Jesus to confess him before humanity (Matthew 10:32; Romans 10:8-10).

Baptism as a symbol of death to oneself (Romans 6:3-14). In salvation, we give up the right to determine the direction of our life and the values by which we want to live. Through baptism, we declare that we have died to ourselves and taken up the values of the new nature which was given to us at conversion. Romans 6 asserts that "we have been buried with Christ" and that we have been "raised ... to live a new life". Having died with him, we shall also live with him.

For this reason, the Mennonite Brethren Church immerses fully; that is, people who are baptized are fully plunged beneath the water to symbolize death to the old life and being raised to a new life.

Baptism as confession of faith. Questions often arise about how soon after conversion a person should be baptized, and how old a person should be before being baptized.

The Bible is silent on the age of baptism. In some church traditions, salvation is immediately followed by baptism regardless of age. In the Mennonite Brethren Church, we follow an unwritten guideline which comes from our understanding of discipleship. Discipleship, the act of following Jesus, is a very intentional choice. To declare that "Jesus is Lord" is, by definition, an adult act. It requires a rather mature understanding of humanity, God and salvation.

In no way does this discredit the work of the Holy Spirit in the lives of young children; rather, it acknowledges that, somewhere in life, a personal, mature affirmation to follow Jesus, regardless of consequences, needs to be made.

Baptism and church membership. In the Mennonite Brethren tradition, baptism and church public membership are linked together. We have already seen that the local church is the visible body of Christ on earth. Therefore, it is natural that when a person becomes a part of God's household through salvation, there should be a commitment to a local church.

In the Mennonite Brethren Church, baptism is a requirement for membership, and when persons are baptized, they are accepted into the membership of the congregation.

Issues facing persons considering baptism

There are many believers who either do not accept baptism and church membership, or if they do, do it with reluctance. Listed below are some of the more common reasons given for not being baptized and joining the local church.

"I don't want to be baptized because I'm not good enough to join the church." Some Christians have come to think that baptism is only for those who have spiritual maturity and are good enough to be part of the church.

Baptism is not a sign that maturity has come; it is a sign that maturity is on its way. To be sure, it is to be expected that signs of emerging maturity are coming into being, but one doesn't have to be perfect to be baptized.

"Why should I be baptized if baptism doesn't add anything to my salvation?" This is a question which surfaces occasionally. The Mennonite Brethren Church understands baptism to be a voluntary act which symbolizes an inner reality. We are agreed that the Bible teaches that grace is not conferred through baptism. So the question is legitimate. It is also a fair question in light of the fact that some church traditions either do not emphasize baptism or don't practice it at all. While it is true that grace is not imparted through baptism, it is nevertheless an important witness to a person's commitment to Christ and the covenant community. It is a public declaration that a person has pledged loyalty and faithfulness to Christ and to the ministry of the local church. It is a sign that a person, through obedience to Christ, is prepared to be a "team player", working for the good of the whole community, and is submitting to discipline through accountability to the local church.

"Why do I have to speak to the gathered church about my life?" Isn't it enough simply to be baptized? Some churches have a very involved procedure leading to baptism; others have simplified it considerably. At the centre of the baptism is the personal confession of faith. The Mennonite Brethren Church, rightly, has placed the emphasis on the confession of personal faith so that baptism will not become a routine rite of passage at a given age. In our churches, those growing up in the congregation usually are encouraged to be baptized during the high school years. The danger of being baptized "because all my friends are being baptized" is considerable. The personal word of witness is a test of the authentic desire of the person to be baptized and to declare, through symbolic action, allegiance to Jesus Christ and his body, the church.

"What should I put into my testimony? My life has been so boring!" The testimony should include at least three things: First, you should tell, in your own words, how you became a believer in Jesus Christ. Each story of faith is a freedom story. Some are more dramatic; others are less dramatic. The drama, or lack of drama, in our personal freedom story is not the issue. The issue is that freedom has come to us in Christ. For some, this story may have a well-remembered, never-to-be-forgotten beginning; for others, it may be a process. What should be clear is that you know that you have received new life in Christ and that he is Lord of your life.

Second, the personal testimony should show some understanding of what baptism means and how it is related to salvation. If there is no understanding of this symbolic act, it will be meaningless.

Third, the personal word of witness should include some careful thinking about why the candidate is requesting to be baptized. If baptism is little more than a rite of passage, or if it is entered only because the church, the pastor, parents or friends are putting pressure on, then the reasons are not strong enough.

"I belong to the invisible church, the eternal body of Christ; I really don't need the local church, nor do I want to belong to it!" It is amazing how many adults draw a line between the eternal body of Christ to which every believer, living and dead, belongs, and the local church. Some people know they are part of this eternal body, but don't want to identify with the local church, which is the visible expression of that eternal body.

Of course, it is true that faith in Christ grants us a place in the eternal family of God. It is also true that the visible, local church is not the sum total of the body of Christ, but only a part. The whole, however, is made up of the parts — parts that are very visible. There are no invisible parts to the body of Christ. The body of Christ is comprised of persons who live in time and space, in a specific society within a given culture.

EXPRESSING THE COVENANT COMMUNITY: THE LORD'S SUPPER

The second of the two ordinances which the Mennonite Brethren Church understands the Scriptures to teach, is the Lord's Supper, sometimes called communion. As with baptism, there is little disagreement in the Mennonite Brethren Church concerning this ordinance. It has been regularly, and with great blessing, practised in the life of the church for well over a century. This consensus on the Lord's Supper is expressed in Article 9 of the Mennonite Brethren Confession of Faith:

Meaning
The church observes the Lord's Supper, as instituted by Christ. The Supper points to Christ, whose body was broken for us and whose blood was shed to assure salvation for believers and to establish the new covenant.

*In the Supper the church identifies with the life of Christ given for the redemp-
tion of humanity and proclaims the Lord's death until he comes. The Supper
expresses the fellowship and unity of all believers with Christ. It is a supper
of remembrance, celebration and praise which strengthens believers for true
discipleship and service.*

Practice

*In preparation for the fellowship of the Lord's Supper, all believers examine
themselves. All those who understand its meaning, confess Jesus Christ as
Lord in word and life, are accountable to their congregation and are living in
right relationship with God and others are invited to participate in the Lord's
Supper. The normal pattern in the New Testament was that baptism preceded
participation in the Lord's Supper.*

The historical setting of the Lord's Supper

The Lord's Supper has a long history, dating back to when Israel was in Egypt.
The deliverance of Israel from slavery was effected by a series of dramatic
events (the Ten Plagues) in which God defeated Pharaoh, the ruler of Egypt
(Exodus 7-12). The final act in this dramatic showdown between God and
Pharaoh was the occasion for the founding of the Passover meal. It was to be
a "lasting ordinance", with no ending (Exodus 12:14).

In the Passover meal, a lamb without defect was slaughtered and eaten. The
blood was caught and swabbed onto the outside of the main door leading into
and out of the house. The Book of Exodus describes a terrible act of judgment
in which a death angel circulated throughout the land and struck dead the
first-born of every home where blood was absent, If the blood was present on
the door, those who resided behind the blood-covering were spared.

Israel was to re-enact this Passover night meal once a year, on the anniver-
sary of this event. Israel was also instructed to pass on to each following
generation the meaning and reason for this meal. By the time Jesus and his
disciples gathered to eat the Passover meal, it had already been practiced for
almost 2,000 years.

Jesus, the disciples and the Passover meal

Three of the four Gospels record the story of the final Passover meal which
Jesus ate with his disciples on the night of his betrayal by Judas Iscariot
(Matthew 26:26-30; Mark 14:22-26; Luke 22:14-20). Paul the Apostle also
recounts the story, claiming it was given to him by special revelation
(1 Corinthians 11:23-25).

As was the custom, Jesus and his disciples ate bread and drank wine with the Passover meal. Fully aware of his impending death, Jesus passed around the bread and said, "Take and eat; this is my body." He took a cup of wine and said, "Drink from it, all of you. This is my blood of the covenant, which is poured out for many for the forgiveness of sins." With these words, he altered the focus of the Passover meal. He changed it from an Old Testament sacrifice in which every year a lamb without blemish was slain to be an atoning death for sins. From now on, the meal would symbolize his own death, which would forever end the need for a lamb to be offered. He, in fact, was God's perfect lamb (John 1:29; Revelation 5:5-6). The focus of the Old Testament story is liberation from slavery in Egypt. The focus of the New Testament story is liberation from the bondage of sin.

The meaning of Jesus' communion words

Jesus made four statements to his disciples at the Passover meal.

The first word. The first saying of Jesus at the Passover meal concerned the matter of betrayal. His comment that someone in this close-knit band of disciples would betray him caused considerable consternation and self-doubt within the group. Each asked the Master, "Surely, not I?" The Scriptures point the finger at Judas Iscariot. Jesus then called on him to do quickly what he intended to do.

The second and third words. The second and third statements are *"Take and eat; this is my body"* (Matthew 26:26) and *"Drink from it, all of you. This is my blood of the covenant, which is poured for many for the forgiveness of sins"* (Matthew 26:27-28).

There are two major views of how these words should be understood. Some believe that in the Lord's Supper, when the bread is broken, blessed and distributed, and when the wine is blessed and distributed, it becomes literally the body and blood of Christ. Adding weight to this understanding is another saying of Jesus. Jesus spoke some very alarming words to his followers — words that were so hard to accept that many decided not to follow him any longer: *"Very truly I tell you, unless you eat the flesh of the Son of Man and drink his blood, you have no life in you. Whoever eats my flesh and drinks my blood has eternal life, and I will raise them up at the last day. For my flesh is real food and my blood is real drink."* (John 6:53-55)

The second main way of viewing these words is to treat them as a metaphor. That is, these words do not represent a literal reality in the sense that Jesus Christ is present bodily at the Lord's Supper; rather, they represent symbolically the presence of Jesus Christ at the Lord's Supper through the Holy Spirit, who is also called "the Spirit of Christ" (2 Corinthians 3:17). In this view, the bread remains the bread, the grape juice/wine remains grape juice/wine. However, Christ is present through the Holy Spirit who, Jesus promised, will always be present wherever and whenever the church gathers (Matthew 18:20).

The Mennonite Brethren Church understands these words in the latter sense. It is Jesus' meal. It is he who invites us, the body of Christ, to his table. He is present, but he is not present bodily. He is present within us because we are the temple in which he lives (1 Corinthians 6:19). He is present at this commemorative meal in the same way as he is present with us in all the circumstances of life (Matthew 28:20b).

The fourth word. The fourth saying of Jesus at the Passover meal stresses the continuity between the past, present and future. Jesus said, *"I tell you, I will not drink of this fruit of the vine from now on until that day when I drink it new with you in my Father's kingdom"* (Matthew 26:29).

At the inception of the Passover meal in Egypt, God promised that this celebration would have no ending. At the Passover meal with the disciples, Jesus instructed his disciples to "do this in remembrance of me" (Luke 22:19), thereby giving the Supper continuity to the end of time. He then promised that this celebration would continue in heaven. In heaven, all believers will drink new wine with Christ. We will celebrate the completion of the atonement of Christ.

In the past, the Israelites commemorated liberation from slavery and physical bondage through the death of a sacrificial lamb. During this present age, as the church gathers around the Lord's Supper, we celebrate Christ's victory over sin and death. And in the great coming day, we will be present with Christ to celebrate forever the ultimate, final victory of God over evil and death.

What does this mean for us?

The Lord's Supper is rich in symbolic meaning for us. Three things flow out of the Gospel texts — things which are also picked up by Paul in the I Corinthians text. Here they are:

It is a time of reflection and self-examination. The Lord's Supper, primarily, is not a party. It is a reflective time of meditating on the meaning of the atoning death of Christ. It is a time of looking inward and of giving thanks to God for "his unspeakable gift" (2 Corinthians 9:15). Paul cautions the Christian church to be careful not to eat and drink damnation to itself through unworthy participation (1 Corinthians 11:27-28).

It is a time when Christ is present in the gathered body, the church. The Lord's Supper is also a time when we celebrate. When Christ is present with and in his gathered body, the local church, it is a time to bask in the knowledge, fellowship and joy of that presence. The Lord's Supper is appropriately named. It is the Lord's table, not ours. We are his guests. We are there to enjoy his presence by his indwelling Spirit.

It is also a time of hope concerning the future. For most of the history of the church, times have been difficult. It is only in the recent past, and largely in the Western world, that peace and prosperity have come to the church. Hope is a light which burns most brightly in the darkness of the night. Hope, in biblical terms, is not a dreamy, pleasant wish about the future; it is a solid reality founded on the promises and words of Jesus Christ (1 Peter 1:3-5). When Christ promised his disciples that he would drink new wine with them in his Father's presence, it sustained them and the early church through very difficult times.

Who is invited to the Lord's Table?

This question has a simple and a more complex answer. The simple answer is: Every person who has received the gift of grace through Christ is invited to the Lord's Supper. The Lord's Supper celebrates the level ground on which every person stands; every person who heeds the invitation "to eat and to drink" in memory of salvation, has come into God's household exactly the same Way — through grace. At the Lord's Supper, every person is equal. No one is better than the next; no one is less important than someone else. Young and old, educated and uneducated, woman and man, "Greek and barbarian" — every person comes to offer thanks to God for the gift of salvation.

The longer answer concerns age and maturity. The Mennonite Brethren Church, having arrived at a consensus which is stated in the Confession of Faith, gives some guidance so that abuse of this symbolic act will not occur. It sets out four conditions to participation: "All who understand its meaning, confess Jesus Christ as Lord in word and deed, are accountable to their congregation and are living in right relationship with God and others are invited to participate in the Lord's Supper."

NOTES:

NOTES:

chapter five
The Mennonite Brethren family

The Mennonite Brethren Church is a worldwide church with its beginnings rooted in the radical reformation of the sixteenth century.

The Anabaptist movement

In the sixteenth century, well-known reformers such as Martin Luther, John Calvin and Ulrich Zwingli called for a return to the faith of the New Testament. These reformers initiated what has become known as the Protestant Reformation.

Lesser known was the call for an even more radical return to the teaching of the New Testament by reformers such as Menno Simons and Conrad Grebel. These men of God called for a renewal of the inner spirit through the new birth, and for strict obedience to the New Testament teachings. The public witness of the new birth was to be believer's baptism. In Europe, where most persons had been baptized as infants, this called for a re-baptism on the basis of an adult confession of faith in Christ. Because of this, the adherents of this movement were soon dubbed "Anabaptists" (the prefix "ana" means "again", and "baptist" means "to be baptized").

One of the early converts to this radical New Testament faith was a Roman Catholic priest named Menno Simons. He became a powerful influence for the movement, drawing many people to faith in Christ. Although the members of the new movement simply called themselves "brothers" or "Christians", they soon were nicknamed "Mennonites" because of the influence of Menno Simons. The label stuck. To this day, Anabaptists are usually called Mennonites.

Missionary zeal was strong, and soon the Anabaptists were everywhere: in Switzerland, Germany and the Netherlands. At the heart of this movement were seven important principles of belief:

Biblical authority. The Anabaptists accepted the Scriptures, and especially the teachings of Jesus, as the final authority on all matters of faith and life. They relegated the authority of the church to a lesser role. The church speaks with authority, they argued, only when it accurately reflects the teachings of the New Testament.

Committed discipleship. A life of faith was to be a life of discipleship, with all of life lived under the lordship of Jesus Christ. Commitment to Christ was understood to imply a life of obedience to all that Jesus had commanded.

Meaningful membership in the church. The church was to be a voluntary community of believers who joined the church on confession of faith in Christ, symbolized by baptism.

Redemptive discipline. The rule of Christ in personal and corporate life led the Anabaptists to exercise a redemptive discipline to win back those who erred from the faith. The intent of discipline was not to punish but to restore.

Mutual concern. The Anabaptists insisted that genuine Christian fellowship must include a mutual concern for the welfare of other church members. A part of this concern was expressed through the sharing of material goods.

Borderless mission. The Anabaptists taught that the love of Christ did not know boundaries and that the Great Commission compelled every believer to be a witness to the gospel of peace. In Christ, all barriers were to come down; in Christ, the fellowship of believers was to transcend national and international boundaries.

Suffering love. The Anabaptists were convinced that Jesus taught the way of peace, and that radical discipleship must express itself in suffering love and nonresistance.

Persecution for these beliefs was intense. Anabaptist believers could easily be identified because they called on new converts to bear bold witness to their new-found faith in Christ through baptism. Because of this, the Mennonites, as they were now called, sought places to live where the persecution would be less rigorous. Some moved to Poland and to Prussia and finally to southern Russia, negotiating with more compliant governments on matters of education, local government and religious freedom. Exemption from military service was always an important factor.

At the same time, the spiritual fervor and vitality were beginning to wane. Missionary zeal became less important than a safe place to live. As wealth accumulated, the practice of radical discipleship also began to become less important.

Mennonite Brethren origins

The Mennonite Brethren Church came into being during a spiritual renewal which swept through southern Russia in the mid-nineteenth century. On January 6, 1860, after a period of intense Bible study and spiritual renewal, eighteen Mennonite families formed a new church dedicated to the principles of New Testament faith.

Through this new beginning, deep devotion to the teachings of the Scriptures and missionary zeal returned to the church. In twelve years, this group grew to over six hundred members. Two new emphases were added to the Anabaptist distinctives: First, conversion was seen to be usually a crisis experience rather than a process, and baptism by immersion (as distinct from the baptism by pouring practiced by the mother Mennonite church) was introduced. Second, nurture and mission were highlighted. Sunday schools were introduced; audible, public prayer was encouraged; gospel songs and youth meetings were instituted; and yearly evangelistic services were stressed. The new group called themselves Mennonite "Brethren" (Brothers) because of the intimate christian fellowship they developed. They treated each other as members of the same loving christian "family".

In the late nineteenth century, the Mennonites (including the Mennonite Brethren) moved again, this time to North and South America. In the 1870's, a large contingent of Mennonites settled in Kansas and from there moved to North and South Dakota, California and Saskatchewan.

In the mid 1920's, another large group emigrated to South America and Canada. Approximately 12,000 Mennonites settled on the Canadian prairies, where they once again found peace. They went about the business of settling into a new land and culture. They built schools and hospitals; they initiated an overseas missions program; they banded together with other Mennonite groups to send relief to peoples all over the world.

The Mennonite Brethren Church today

From such small beginnings, a church has emerged which spans the world. According to ICOMB – the International Community of Mennonite Brethren – there are 19 national fellowships ("Conferences") with over 2200 congregations (and many more outreach cells or 'preaching points') and almost 400,000 members in our world wide family. And the church continues to grow. The Mennonite Brethren church family extends to Africa, Asia, Europe and Latin America. The largest group is in India where membership is approaching 200,000.

In North America, there are approximately 450 congregations with close to 70,000 members. These churches also worship in many languages, including Spanish, French, Vietnamese, Chinese, Arabic, Hmong, Slavic, Portuguese, Hindi/Punjabi, German and English. Church planting continues to be a high priority in all regions of North America and overseas.

MB Mission, the global mission organization, leads the way to transform lives through mission. They prioritize planting churches in unreached areas of the world. ICOMB has been established as a fellowship of leaders from established national conferences. They meet annually to support one another and plan programs to serve the global Mennonite Brethren church.

Doing together what we can't do alone

The Mennonite Brethren church family has learned that there is value in working together on projects, so that through our collective strength we can do together what we can't do alone. Most of this work is done through regional groupings of churches called "conferences". In Canada, there are six provincial conferences (B.C., Alberta, Saskatchewan., Manitoba, Ontario and Quebec) and an emerging conference in the Atlantic provinces. In the U.S., there are five district conferences, three of which are defined by a cluster of states (Pacific, Central and Southern), and two which lie predominantly within an individual state: the Latin American (Texas) and North Carolina conferences. Each of these conferences meets annually in convention to give structure and accountability for joint projects such as schools, camps, church planting and congregational care ministries. Details of these ministries are available in convention yearbooks.

The Canadian churches and the U.S. churches also band together to work at national issues. In each country, delegates meet every other year to hear national staff present accountability reports and to decide on programs that serve local churches.

The Mennonite Brethren churches and conferences also co-operate with many other agencies to do the work of the Kingdom of God. The Mennonite Brethren church holds firmly to an integrative theological position which must express itself in both winning people to Christ (the Great Commission) and in helping those in need (the Great Commandment). The Mennonite Central Committee (MCC) is the relief and development arm of the church, bringing the Mennonite Brethren church together in partnership with all of the other Mennonite denominations. MCC is active in worldwide relief, in development projects and in disaster aid. Together with the co-operating Mennonite denominations, it has become a strong witness to the way of peace.

Conclusion

The Mennonite Brethren family is diverse and continues to grow. It has reached well beyond its roots to become an international family. It works in harmony and partnership to bring about the growth of the Kingdom of God.

NOTES:

For further study:

Bonhoeffer, Dietrich. *Life Together: The Classic Exploration of Faith in Community.* New York, NY: HarperOne: 1978.

Confession of Faith: Commentary and Pastoral Application. Winnipeg, MB: Kindred Productions: 2002.

Foster, Richard. *Celebration of Discipline: The Path to Spiritual Growth.* New York, NY: HarperOne: 1988.

Heidebrecht, Doug. *Interpreting the Bible Together.* DVD Curriculum. Winnipeg, MB: Kindred Productions: 2006.

Jost, Lynn and Connie Faber. *Family Matters: Discovering the Mennonite Brethren.* Winnipeg, MB: Kindred Productions: 2002.

Martens, Elmer A. and Peter J. Klassen, eds. *Knowing & Living Your Faith: A Study on the Confession of Faith.* ICOMB International Community of Mennonite Brethren. Winnipeg, MB: Kindred Productions: 2008.

Neufeld, Alfred. *What We Believe Together: Exploring the "Shared Convictions of Anabaptist-Related Churches.* Intercourse, PA: Good Books: 2008.

Packer, J.I. *Knowing God.* Downers Grove, IL: InterVarsity Press: 1993.

LEADER'S GUIDE

The leader's guide is a tool to help you teach *New Life In Christ* in a membership class setting. The questions, optional videos and suggestions for local church input will all need to be shaped into a meaningful lesson plan for your unique situation. The questions serve as a starting point and as you develop your lesson plans you will undoubtedly think of others that you want to include. The lessons that follow are intended to lead a class through the basics of Christian faith, an understanding of church life, including the local church setting, and a brief introduction to the larger Mennonite Brethren family and history.

The five lessons correspond to the chapter divisions of the manual. The duration of the study can be adapted to fit your local church structure for membership classes.

Throughout your sessions together as a group encourage the participants to continue reading the membership manual. It will broaden their understanding and contribute to a fuller class discussion.

NOTE: The *MB Confession of Faith* and the resources mentioned throughout the leader's guide are available from:

KINDRED PRODCTIONS
1-800-545-7322
www.kindredproductions.com

Your church library or local Conference Resource Center may also have the resources listed or additional material that you will find helpful.

1. Beginning the New Life

Scripture basis: Ephesians 1:3-14; 2:1-10;
Romans 8:1-11, 28-39; John 3:16

Introduce members of the class to one another and interact with them on their expectations regarding the class and your purposes in teaching it.

As you prepare your lesson for *Beginning the New Life* be sure and incorporate question #11. It is important for class members to hear each others stories of faith.

1. Following the lesson introduce the MB Confession of Faith and distribute copies for each class member to read prior to your next class.

2. Why do the Scriptures uniformly teach that all human beings need to be reconciled with God?

3. What is, ultimately, the problem with humanity — is it the sins we commit or is it our separation and alienation from God?

4. Is it possible to become a Christian without God's initiative in the matter?

5. What is the difference between being helplessly lost versus hopelessly lost?

6. What words are used in Scripture to describe salvation? Explain their meaning.

7. Salvation is a gift of God. What happens when we receive the gift of salvation?

8. What is involved in becoming a Christian?

9. What is the difference between becoming a Christian and being a Christian?

10. In your own words give a definition of a Christian? Given your definition are you a Christian?

11. Take a few moments and have class members share their personal story of becoming a Christian. Who influenced them in their decision? How has life changed as a result of becoming a Christian?

12. What assurance do we have that we are indeed Christians?

13. The main privilege that we have as Christians is a personal relationship with God. How can we ensure that our relationship continues to mature?

2. Reading and Understanding the Bible

Scripture basis: 1 Peter 1:23-25; 2 Timothy 3:16-17

The Bible is the foundation for our life of discipleship and service.

The MB Confession of Faith is a statement on how we understand the Bible. Include questions #12 and #13 in your lesson plan. Option: Use the video "Interpreting the Bible Together" for further study (5:X 15-20 minute lessons). Note: Inform the class of your church's procedures for hearing testimonies, baptism and the reception into membership. Also encourage the continued reading of the Membership Manual.

1. What means has God used to communicate with humanity?

2. Discuss the structure of the Bible in terms of Old and New Testaments; number of books; authorship; date; type of literature.

3. What key theme brings unity to the biblical message?

4. Why is it important to recognize the Bible as God's word? What is the significance of the Bible being God's divine word versus a human book?

5. On what basis can we trust the Bible?

6. Why is attitude important in the reading and studying of the Bible?

7. How does the Bible build us up in faith?

8. How have you personally made Bible reading meaningful for your devotional life?

9. What does God expect of us as we read and understand his word? (see James 2:22ff)

10. Why do we develop summary statements about the Bible?

11. What are the strengths and weaknesses of summary statements?

12. Discuss the Confession of Faith and answer questions.

13. Do you think our Confession of Faith is descriptive of our faith, or is it also prescriptive in what it calls us to believe and do?

3. Living the Christian Life

Scripture basis: Romans 12:1-21; Ephesians 6:10-18; Matthew 25:14-30

We live the Christian life in the context of the fellowship of believers in a local church setting. As you prepare your lesson, take note of questions #15 and #16. Make sure that participants understand the structure of your church and the opportunities for service.

1. Why isn't it enough to know about God? Why is it important to know God personally?

2. Why is it necessary for Christians of all ages and all maturity levels to continue to grow in their knowledge of God?

3. Discuss the six disciplines of the spiritual life listed.

4. What are some means of ensuring an effective prayer life?

5. Which spiritual disciplines come most easily to you? Why?

6. Encourage participants to choose a discipline in which they desire to mature and have them develop a plan of action for growth. The practice leads to godly living.

7. What is one of the best arguments for the reality of the gospel?

8. Ethics is the word we use to describe the discernment between what is right and what is wrong. Why do we have more trouble doing what is right than doing what is wrong? (see Romans 7:7-25)

9. What role does accountability play in living the Christian life?

10. What qualities should characterize Christian relationships? (friendship, marriage, parenting, employer/employee, church/state)

11. Why is service such an important part of being a Christian?

12. Discuss the nature of spiritual gifts and their role in the life of the church. (see Romans 12:4-8; 1 Corinthians 12-14; Ephesians 4:11-16; 1 Peter 4:7-11)

13. How would you begin to discern and explore the spiritual gifts that you have as an individual?

14. Discuss the fact that apart from the gift of evangelism, each believing person is to be a faithful witness for Jesus Christ. What are the most challenging aspects in sharing your faith?

15. Take the opportunity to discuss the various ministry positions in your church. Explain the church governance structure and the process for election to service and the appointment of volunteers. If you have a gift inventory for members, have the class complete it.

16. Take the opportunity to discuss stewardship and the responsibilities of church members in financially supporting the ministries of the church. Distribute the church budget and discuss.

4. Living in the Church, the Community of Faith

Scripture basis:

a) Church - 1 Corinthians 12:12-27; Ephesians 4:1-16; 1 Peter 2:4-10

b) Baptism - Matthew 3:13-17; 28:18-20; Romans 6:1-10 Acts 2:38

c) The Lord's Supper - Matthew 26:17-30; 1 Corinthians 11:17-34

In this lesson the goal is to grow in our understanding of the church as a fellowship of believers. In your lesson plan include a discussion of your church's mission statement and membership covenant. Clarify your church's approach to the practice of baptism and the celebration of communion. A clear understanding of the implications of question #9 is important to our Mennonite Brethren understanding of accountability within the fellowship of believers.

The Church

1. Have class members share how the church has had an impact on their family and/or in their personal lives.

2. Discuss the nature of the church and develop a working definition of the church.

3. What would you understand to be the purpose of the church?

4. What constitutes membership in the church?

5. Is it possible to be part of the body of Christ without being part of the local church

Baptism

6. Discuss the responsibilities of members to the church and the church to its members.

7. What does the word baptize mean, and how is it used in regard to water baptism?

8. What are the requirements for baptism? Why should believers be baptized? What is the significance of baptism for the believer?

9. Why are baptism and church membership tied together in our church tradition?

10. In the first century church, conversion and baptism were seen to be two parts — one inner, the other, outer — of the same experience. Baptism followed conversion very closely. Have class members consider their conversion. Discuss: What factors have led you to postpone baptism? What have been the benefits of waiting? How have you grown in your commitment? Is baptism an initiation rite or a graduation certificate? Why? Why not? When is a person old enough to meaningfully make a personal declaration of faith through baptism?

11. Encourage class members to write out their testimony and share it with someone in the next week.

The Lord's Supper

12. Discuss the meaning of the Lord's Supper.

13. Share concerning the significance of the celebration of the Lord's Supper in the worship life of the church.

14. Who is invited to participate in communion?

5. The Mennonite Brethren Family

Our past shapes the present. Understanding the past will help us to discover where we have come from and enable us to set goals for the future. As you teach this lesson help participants gain an understanding of the larger MB family - its history, structure, mission and vision. Also take time to discuss your local church history, mission impact and vision for the future.

1. The Anabaptist movement has its roots in the sixteenth century reformation. What were the distinctive features of Anabaptism?

2. Discuss their significance for the church today.

3. What factors led to the birth of the Mennonite Brethren Church?

4. Discuss the various conference ministries: District/Provincial, National, ICOMB. Distribute conference brochures as available or view websites usmb.org; mbconf.ca; icomb.org and your region's website.

5. Highlight the work of Mennonite Brethren Mission and introduce the class to your church's missionaries.

6. Share the history of your local church with the class.